ANCIENT MYTHOLOGY
EGYPTIAN MYTHS AND LEGENDS

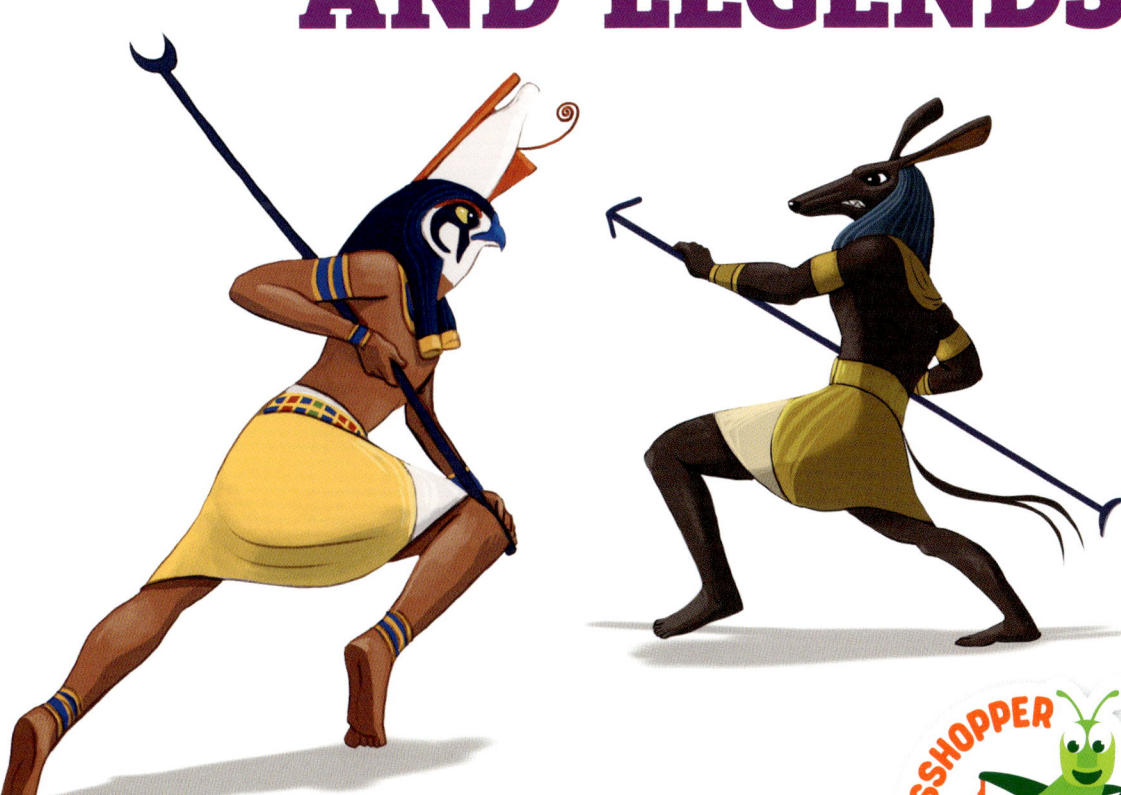

by Alyssa Krekelberg
illustrated by Cesar Samaniego

Tools for Parents & Teachers

Grasshopper Books enhance imagination and introduce the earliest readers to fun storylines and illustrations. The easy-to-read text supports early reading experiences with repetitive sentence patterns and sight words.

Before Reading

- Discuss the cover illustration. What do readers see?
- Look at the glossary together. Discuss the words.

During Reading

- "Walk" through the book with the reader. Discuss new or unfamiliar words. Sound them out together.
- Look at the illustrations. When and where does the story take place? What is happening in the story?

After Reading

- Prompt the child to think more. Ask: What is your favorite Egyptian myth? Why?

Grasshopper Books are published by Jump!
3500 American Blvd W, Suite 150
Bloomington, MN 55431
www.jumplibrary.com

Copyright © 2026 Jump! International copyright reserved in all countries. No part of this book may be reproduced in any form without written permission from the publisher.

Jump! is a division of FlutterBee Education Group.

Library of Congress Cataloging-in-Publication Data

Names: Krekelberg, Alyssa, author.
Samaniego, César, 1975- illustrator.
Title: Egyptian myths and legends / by Alyssa Krekelberg; illustrated by Cesar Samaniego.
Description: Minneapolis, MN: Jump!, Inc., 2026.
Series: Ancient mythology | Includes index.
Audience: Ages 7-10
Identifiers: LCCN 2024044356 (print)
LCCN 2024044357 (ebook)
ISBN 9798892137478 (hardcover)
ISBN 9798892137485 (paperback)
ISBN 9798892137492 (ebook)
Subjects: LCSH: Mythology, Egyptian–Juvenile literature. Gods, Egyptian–Juvenile literature.
Classification: LCC BL2441.3 .K74 2026 (print)
LCC BL2441.3 (ebook)
DDC 398.20932–dc23/eng/20241121
LC record available at https://lccn.loc.gov/2024044356
LC ebook record available at https://lccn.loc.gov/2024044357

Editor: Katie Chanez
Direction and Layout: Anna Peterson
Illustrator: Cesar Samaniego
Content Consultant: Rita Lucarelli, PhD; University of California, Berkeley

Printed in the United States of America at Corporate Graphics in North Mankato, Minnesota.

Table of Contents

Magic and Mummies	4
Egyptian Gods and Goddesses	22
To Learn More	23
Glossary	24
Index	24

Magic and Mummies

At the beginning of time, there was only ocean. Atum rose from the water. He was the Egyptian god of **creation**.

Atum made other gods. These gods had children. Geb was the god of the earth. Nut was the goddess of the sky.

Ancient Egyptians believed gods could change the world around them. Ra was the Sun. He rose each day. Hapy was the Nile River. His waters brought good soil to farms.

Gods took many forms. Some had animal heads. People told stories about them. These stories are known as Egyptian **mythology**.

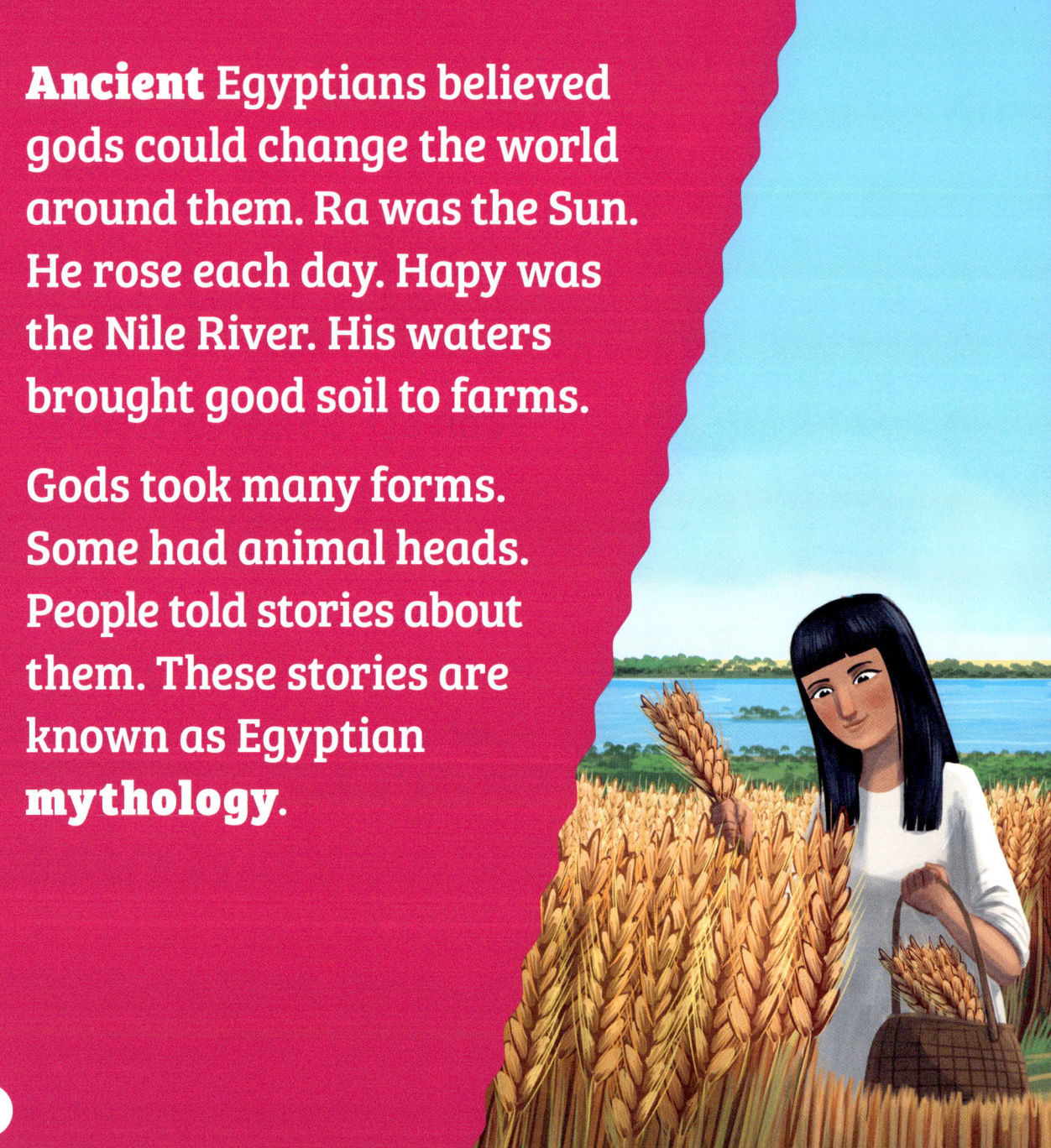

Ra sailed across the sky each day. He brought sunlight to the world.

At night, he sailed through the **underworld**. A giant serpent named Apep attacked him. It wanted to stop the Sun from rising. But Seth protected Ra. Ra rose into the sky each morning.

Seth

Hathor was the goddess of the sky, joy, and love. But when part of her turned into a lion, she became Sekhmet.

Sekhmet ripped up **crops**. She destroyed homes. She wouldn't stop, even when Ra asked! He gave her a special drink. It made her fall asleep. When she woke up, she was the kind and loving Hathor again.

The god Osiris was the first king of Egypt. He taught people how to make bread. He helped them build **temples**. People loved him.

His brother, Seth, was the god of **chaos**. He was jealous of Osiris. He locked Osiris in a coffin. He threw it into the Nile River. Seth then ruled Egypt.

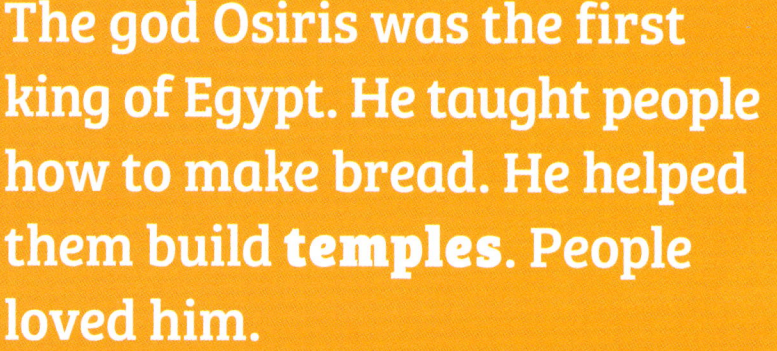

Isis was Osiris's wife. She was the goddess of healing and magic. She found Osiris, but he was dead. She wanted to help him. The god Anubis did, too. He took care of the dead. He wrapped Osiris in cloth. He made Osiris into the first mummy.

Isis poured magic into Osiris. He woke up. But now Osiris was the god of the dead. He had to live in the underworld.

When a person died, they went to the underworld. Anubis guided them to the Hall of Judgment. Here, they had to pass a test to get to the **afterlife**.

Ma'at was the goddess of truth and **justice**. She put a feather on a scale. The person's heart went on the other side. If the person was bad, their heart was heavier than Ma'at's feather. They could not have a peaceful afterlife.

Isis and Osiris had a son named Horus. He was the god of the sky. One day, Seth sent a snake to bite him. Horus was poisoned!

Isis begged the other gods for help. Thoth was the god of wisdom. He gave Isis spells that healed Horus.

Both Horus and Seth wanted to rule Egypt. They had many contests. One time, they raced stone boats. But Horus's boat only looked like stone. It was built out of wood. His boat floated. Seth's stone boat sank. Horus won! Horus became king. Egypt did well under his rule. People praised him!

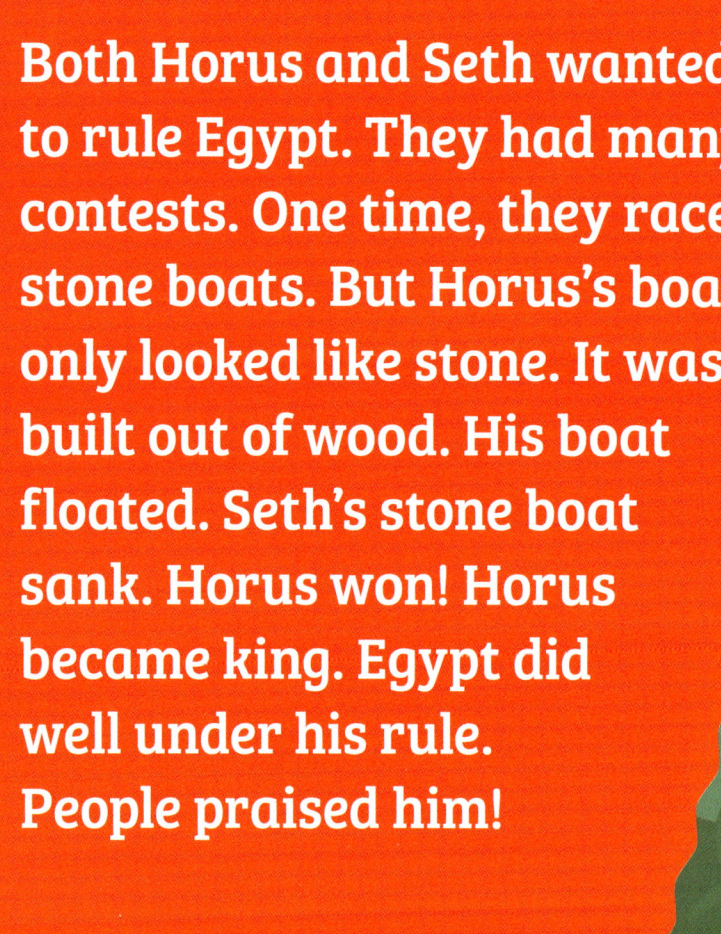

Egyptian Gods and Goddesses

Who are Egyptian mythology's most important gods and goddesses? Take a look!

Anubis
God of mummification and the afterlife

Atum
God of creation

Geb
God of the earth

Hapy
God of the Nile River

Hathor
Goddess of the sky, joy, and love

Horus
God of the sky and kingship

Isis
Goddess of healing and magic

Ma'at
Goddess of truth and justice

Nut
Goddess of the sky

Osiris
God of the dead

Ra
Sun god

Sekhmet
Goddess of war and chaos

Seth
God of chaos

Thoth
God of wisdom

To Learn More

FACT SURFER

Finding more information is as easy as 1, 2, 3.

❶ Go to www.factsurfer.com
❷ Enter "**Egyptianmythsandlegends**" into the search box.
❸ Choose your book to see a list of websites.

Glossary

afterlife: A place where the dead lived happily if they passed Ma'at's test.
ancient: Very old or from the very distant past.
chaos: Complete confusion.
creation: The act of making something.
crops: Plants grown for food.
justice: Fair treatment.
mythology: A group of stories from a particular culture or religion.
temples: Buildings in which gods are worshipped.
underworld: A place in myths where the dead go.

Index

afterlife 16, 17
Anubis 14, 16
Atum 4, 5
Hall of Judgment 16
Hathor 10
Horus 18, 20
Isis 14, 18
Ma'at 17

mummy 14
Nile River 6, 12
Osiris 12, 14, 18
Ra 6, 8, 9, 10
Sekhmet 10
Seth 9, 12, 18, 20
Thoth 18
underworld 9, 14, 16